50 British Tea-Time Treats

By: Kelly Johnson

Table of Contents

- Scones
- Clotted cream
- Strawberry jam
- Victoria sponge
- Battenberg cake
- Eccles cakes
- Bakewell tart
- Jam tarts
- Treacle tart
- Custard tarts
- Chelsea buns
- Lardy cake
- Parkin
- Shortbread
- Flapjacks
- Rock cakes
- Welsh cakes
- Scottish tablet
- Dundee cake
- Bara brith
- Cornish fairings
- Seed cake
- Gingerbread
- Macaroons
- Viennese whirls
- Jaffa cakes
- Bourbon biscuits
- Custard creams
- Digestive biscuits
- Rich tea biscuits
- Hobnobs
- Garibaldi biscuits
- Malt loaf
- Madeira cake
- Lemon drizzle cake

- Carrot cake
- Sticky toffee pudding
- Apple crumble
- Jam roly-poly
- Spotted dick
- Bread and butter pudding
- Queen of puddings
- Tea loaf
- Fat rascals
- Banbury cakes
- Maids of honour tarts
- Yorkshire curd tart
- Cornish splits
- Ginger snaps
- Brandy snaps

Classic Scones

Ingredients:

- 2 cups (250g) all-purpose flour
- 1/4 cup (50g) granulated sugar
- 1 tbsp baking powder
- 1/2 tsp salt
- 1/2 cup (113g) unsalted butter, cold and cubed
- 1/2 cup (120ml) heavy cream (plus extra for brushing)
- 1 large egg
- 1 tsp vanilla extract

Optional Add-ins:

- 1/2 cup raisins, chocolate chips, or berries
- Zest of 1 lemon or orange

Instructions:

1. **Preheat oven** to 400°F (200°C) and line a baking sheet with parchment paper.
2. **Mix dry ingredients:** In a large bowl, whisk together flour, sugar, baking powder, and salt.
3. **Cut in butter:** Add cold butter cubes and cut them into the flour using a pastry cutter or your fingers until the mixture resembles coarse crumbs.
4. **Mix wet ingredients:** In a separate bowl, whisk together the heavy cream, egg, and vanilla.
5. **Combine:** Pour the wet ingredients into the dry ingredients and mix until just combined. Do not overwork the dough. If adding mix-ins, fold them in now.
6. **Shape the dough:** Transfer the dough to a floured surface and gently knead it a few times. Pat into a 1-inch thick circle and cut into 8 wedges.
7. **Bake:** Place scones on the prepared baking sheet, brush with heavy cream, and bake for 15-18 minutes or until golden brown.
8. **Cool & Serve:** Let cool slightly and serve warm with butter, jam, or clotted cream.

Clotted Cream

Ingredients:

- 2 cups (480ml) heavy cream (not ultra-pasteurized)

Instructions:

1. Preheat oven to 180°F (82°C). Pour cream into a shallow baking dish (the wider, the better).
2. Bake for 10-12 hours until a thick, yellowish crust forms on top.
3. Let cool, then refrigerate for at least 8 hours.
4. Skim off the thick clotted cream and stir before serving.

Strawberry Jam

Ingredients:

- 2 cups (400g) strawberries, hulled and chopped
- 1 1/2 cups (300g) granulated sugar
- 1 tbsp lemon juice

Instructions:

1. In a saucepan, combine strawberries, sugar, and lemon juice.
2. Cook over medium heat, stirring occasionally, until the sugar dissolves.
3. Bring to a simmer and cook for 20-25 minutes until thickened.
4. Let cool, then store in sterilized jars.

Victoria Sponge Cake

Ingredients:

For the sponge:

- 1 cup (225g) unsalted butter, softened
- 1 cup (225g) granulated sugar
- 4 large eggs
- 2 cups (225g) self-rising flour
- 1 tsp vanilla extract
- 2 tbsp milk

For the filling:

- 1/2 cup (120ml) heavy cream, whipped
- 1/2 cup strawberry jam
- Powdered sugar for dusting

Instructions:

1. Preheat oven to 350°F (180°C). Grease and line two 8-inch cake tins.
2. Beat butter and sugar until light and fluffy.
3. Add eggs one at a time, then mix in vanilla.
4. Fold in flour and milk until combined.
5. Divide batter between tins and bake for 20-25 minutes.
6. Let cool, then spread jam and cream between layers. Dust with powdered sugar.

Battenberg Cake

Ingredients:

For the cake:

- 1 cup (225g) unsalted butter, softened
- 1 cup (225g) granulated sugar
- 4 large eggs
- 2 cups (225g) self-rising flour
- 1 tsp vanilla extract
- 1/2 tsp almond extract
- Red or pink food coloring

For assembly:

- 1/2 cup (150g) apricot jam
- 1 lb (450g) marzipan
- Powdered sugar (for dusting)

Instructions:

1. Preheat oven to 350°F (180°C). Grease and line an 8-inch square cake tin.
2. Beat butter and sugar until fluffy, then mix in eggs one at a time.
3. Fold in flour and extracts until smooth.
4. Divide batter in half; color one half pink.
5. Bake each half in separate sections of the tin for 25-30 minutes.
6. Once cool, trim and cut each cake into two long strips.
7. Warm apricot jam and use it to stick the strips together in a checkerboard pattern.
8. Roll marzipan out, wrap the cake, and smooth the edges.

Eccles Cakes

Ingredients:

- 1 sheet puff pastry, thawed
- 1/2 cup (75g) currants
- 1/4 cup (50g) brown sugar
- 1/2 tsp cinnamon
- 1/4 tsp nutmeg
- 1 tbsp butter, melted
- 1 egg white, beaten (for glazing)
- Granulated sugar (for sprinkling)

Instructions:

1. Preheat oven to 400°F (200°C). Line a baking sheet with parchment paper.
2. Mix currants, brown sugar, cinnamon, nutmeg, and melted butter.
3. Roll out puff pastry and cut into circles (about 4 inches).
4. Place a spoonful of filling in the center of each circle. Fold edges over and seal.
5. Flip, press gently to flatten, brush with egg white, and sprinkle with sugar.
6. Bake for 15-20 minutes until golden.

Bakewell Tart

Ingredients:

For the pastry:

- 1 1/4 cups (160g) all-purpose flour
- 1/2 cup (115g) butter, cold and cubed
- 2 tbsp powdered sugar
- 1 egg yolk
- 1-2 tbsp cold water

For the filling:

- 1/4 cup (80g) raspberry jam
- 1/2 cup (115g) butter, softened
- 1/2 cup (100g) granulated sugar
- 2 large eggs
- 1 cup (100g) ground almonds
- 1/2 tsp almond extract
- 1/4 cup (25g) sliced almonds

Instructions:

1. Preheat oven to 375°F (190°C). Grease a tart tin.
2. Rub butter into flour and sugar, then mix in egg yolk and water to form dough. Chill for 30 min.
3. Roll out and line the tart tin, then blind bake for 15 min.
4. Spread jam over the base.
5. Beat butter and sugar, then add eggs, almonds, and almond extract. Spread over the jam.
6. Sprinkle with sliced almonds and bake for 30-35 min until golden.

Jam Tarts

Ingredients:

- 1 1/4 cups (160g) all-purpose flour
- 1/2 cup (115g) butter, cold and cubed
- 2 tbsp powdered sugar
- 1 egg yolk
- 1-2 tbsp cold water
- 1/2 cup (120g) jam (strawberry, raspberry, or apricot)

Instructions:

1. Preheat oven to 375°F (190°C). Grease a muffin tin.
2. Rub butter into flour and sugar, then mix in egg yolk and water to form dough. Chill for 30 min.
3. Roll out and cut circles to fit into muffin tin.
4. Spoon a little jam into each tart (don't overfill).
5. Bake for 12-15 min until golden.

Treacle Tart

Ingredients:

For the pastry:

- 1 1/4 cups (160g) all-purpose flour
- 1/2 cup (115g) butter, cold and cubed
- 1 tbsp sugar
- 1 egg yolk
- 1-2 tbsp cold water

For the filling:

- 1 1/4 cups (300g) golden syrup
- 1 cup (100g) fresh breadcrumbs
- 2 tbsp lemon juice
- 1 egg, beaten

Instructions:

1. Preheat oven to 375°F (190°C). Grease a tart tin.
2. Make pastry by rubbing butter into flour and sugar, then mix in egg yolk and water. Chill for 30 min.
3. Roll out and line the tart tin, then blind bake for 15 min.
4. Mix golden syrup, breadcrumbs, lemon juice, and egg. Pour into tart case.
5. Bake for 30 min until golden.

Custard Tarts

Ingredients:

- 1 sheet puff pastry, thawed
- 1 cup (250ml) heavy cream
- 2 egg yolks
- 1/4 cup (50g) sugar
- 1/2 tsp vanilla extract
- Ground nutmeg

Instructions:

1. Preheat oven to 375°F (190°C). Grease a muffin tin.
2. Roll out pastry and cut circles to fit tin.
3. Whisk cream, egg yolks, sugar, and vanilla. Pour into pastry cases.
4. Sprinkle with nutmeg and bake for 20-25 min until set.

Chelsea Buns

Ingredients:

- 3 1/2 cups (450g) bread flour
- 1/4 cup (50g) sugar
- 1 tsp salt
- 1 packet (7g) yeast
- 3/4 cup (180ml) warm milk
- 1/4 cup (60g) butter, melted
- 1 egg
- 1/2 cup (100g) brown sugar
- 1 tsp cinnamon
- 1/2 cup (75g) raisins
- 2 tbsp honey

Instructions:

1. Mix flour, sugar, salt, and yeast. Add milk, butter, and egg. Knead for 10 min. Let rise for 1 hr.
2. Roll dough into a rectangle. Spread with brown sugar, cinnamon, and raisins. Roll up and cut into slices.
3. Place in a baking dish and let rise for 30 min.
4. Bake at 375°F (190°C) for 25 min. Brush with warm honey.

Lardy Cake

Ingredients:

- 3 1/2 cups (450g) bread flour
- 1/2 cup (120g) lard (or butter)
- 1/4 cup (50g) sugar
- 1 tsp salt
- 1 packet (7g) yeast
- 3/4 cup (180ml) warm water
- 1/2 cup (75g) raisins
- 1 tsp cinnamon

Instructions:

1. Mix flour, yeast, sugar, and salt. Add warm water and knead for 10 min. Let rise for 1 hr.
2. Roll out, spread lard, sugar, cinnamon, and raisins. Fold and repeat.
3. Shape into a loaf, let rise for 30 min, then bake at 375°F (190°C) for 35-40 min.

Parkin

Ingredients:

- 1 cup (250g) oatmeal
- 1 cup (125g) self-rising flour
- 1/2 cup (100g) brown sugar
- 1 tsp ginger
- 1/2 tsp cinnamon
- 1/2 cup (120g) butter
- 3/4 cup (180ml) golden syrup
- 1 egg
- 1/4 cup (60ml) milk

Instructions:

1. Preheat oven to 325°F (160°C). Grease a baking tin.
2. Melt butter, sugar, and syrup together.
3. Mix dry ingredients, then add wet mixture, egg, and milk.
4. Pour into tin and bake for 45 min.

Shortbread

Ingredients:

- 1 cup (225g) butter, softened
- 1/2 cup (100g) sugar
- 2 cups (250g) all-purpose flour

Instructions:

1. Preheat oven to 325°F (160°C). Line a baking sheet.
2. Beat butter and sugar, then mix in flour.
3. Press into a baking dish, score with a knife, and bake for 30 min.

Flapjacks

Ingredients:

- 1/2 cup (120g) butter
- 1/2 cup (100g) brown sugar
- 1/2 cup (120ml) golden syrup
- 2 1/2 cups (250g) oats

Instructions:

1. Preheat oven to 350°F (180°C). Grease a baking tin.
2. Melt butter, sugar, and syrup. Stir in oats.
3. Press into tin and bake for 20 min.

Rock Cakes

Ingredients:

- 2 cups (250g) flour
- 1/2 cup (100g) sugar
- 1/2 cup (115g) butter
- 1 egg
- 3 tbsp milk
- 1/2 cup (75g) raisins

Instructions:

1. Preheat oven to 375°F (190°C). Grease a baking sheet.
2. Rub butter into flour and sugar. Add egg, milk, and raisins.
3. Drop spoonfuls onto sheet and bake for 15 min.

Welsh Cakes

Ingredients:

- 2 cups (250g) self-rising flour
- 1/2 cup (115g) butter, cold and cubed
- 1/4 cup (50g) sugar
- 1/2 cup (75g) currants or raisins
- 1 egg
- 2 tbsp milk
- 1/2 tsp mixed spice (optional)

Instructions:

1. Rub butter into flour until crumbly. Stir in sugar, currants, and spice.
2. Beat egg with milk and mix into dry ingredients to form a dough.
3. Roll out to 1/4 inch thick and cut into circles.
4. Cook on a greased griddle or frying pan over medium heat for 2-3 minutes per side until golden.
5. Sprinkle with sugar and serve warm.

Scottish Tablet

Ingredients:

- 2 cups (400g) sugar
- 1/2 cup (120ml) milk
- 1/2 cup (115g) butter
- 1 can (397g) sweetened condensed milk

Instructions:

1. Heat sugar, milk, and butter in a pan over low heat until melted.
2. Add condensed milk and bring to a boil, stirring continuously.
3. Simmer for 20 min, stirring, until golden and thick.
4. Beat for a few minutes until the mixture thickens.
5. Pour into a greased tin and let set before cutting into squares.

Dundee Cake

Ingredients:

- 1 cup (225g) butter, softened
- 1 cup (225g) sugar
- 4 large eggs
- 2 cups (250g) all-purpose flour
- 1 tsp baking powder
- 1/2 cup (75g) ground almonds
- 1 cup (150g) mixed dried fruit
- 1/4 cup (50g) glace cherries, halved
- Zest of 1 orange
- 1/4 cup (50g) blanched almonds (for topping)

Instructions:

1. Preheat oven to 325°F (160°C). Grease and line an 8-inch cake tin.
2. Cream butter and sugar, then add eggs one at a time.
3. Fold in flour, baking powder, ground almonds, dried fruit, cherries, and zest.
4. Pour into tin, arrange almonds on top, and bake for 1.5-2 hours until a skewer comes out clean.

Bara Brith

Ingredients:

- 2 cups (300g) mixed dried fruit
- 1 cup (240ml) strong tea
- 1 cup (200g) brown sugar
- 2 cups (250g) self-rising flour
- 1 tsp mixed spice
- 1 egg

Instructions:

1. Soak dried fruit in tea overnight.
2. Preheat oven to 350°F (180°C). Grease a loaf tin.
3. Stir sugar, flour, spice, and egg into the soaked fruit.
4. Pour into the tin and bake for 1 hour.

Cornish Fairings

Ingredients:

- 1 cup (125g) all-purpose flour
- 1/2 tsp baking soda
- 1/2 tsp cinnamon
- 1/2 tsp ginger
- 1/4 cup (50g) butter
- 1/4 cup (50g) sugar
- 2 tbsp golden syrup

Instructions:

1. Preheat oven to 375°F (190°C). Line a baking sheet.
2. Rub butter into flour, baking soda, and spices.
3. Stir in sugar, then mix in golden syrup to form a dough.
4. Roll into small balls, place on the sheet, and bake for 10-12 min.

Seed Cake

Ingredients:

- 1 cup (225g) butter, softened
- 1 cup (200g) sugar
- 4 large eggs
- 2 cups (250g) all-purpose flour
- 1 tsp baking powder
- 1 tbsp caraway seeds

Instructions:

1. Preheat oven to 350°F (180°C). Grease a loaf tin.
2. Cream butter and sugar, then beat in eggs.
3. Fold in flour, baking powder, and caraway seeds.
4. Pour into the tin and bake for 45-50 min.

Gingerbread

Ingredients:

- 2 cups (250g) all-purpose flour
- 1/2 cup (100g) brown sugar
- 1 tsp ginger
- 1 tsp cinnamon
- 1/2 tsp baking soda
- 1/2 cup (120g) butter
- 1/2 cup (120ml) molasses
- 1/2 cup (120ml) milk

Instructions:

1. Preheat oven to 350°F (180°C). Grease a baking dish.
2. Mix flour, sugar, spices, and baking soda.
3. Melt butter and mix with molasses and milk. Stir into dry ingredients.
4. Pour into dish and bake for 30 min.

Macaroons

Ingredients:

- 2 cups (200g) shredded coconut
- 2/3 cup (130g) sugar
- 2 egg whites
- 1 tsp vanilla extract

Instructions:

1. Preheat oven to 325°F (160°C). Line a baking sheet.
2. Mix coconut, sugar, egg whites, and vanilla.
3. Drop spoonfuls onto the sheet and bake for 15-18 min.

Viennese Whirls

Ingredients:

- 1 cup (225g) butter, softened
- 1/2 cup (60g) powdered sugar
- 1 1/4 cups (150g) flour
- 1/2 cup (60g) cornstarch
- 1/2 tsp vanilla extract

For filling:

- 1/2 cup (120g) butter, softened
- 1 cup (120g) powdered sugar
- 1/4 cup (80g) raspberry jam

Instructions:

1. Preheat oven to 375°F (190°C). Line a baking sheet.
2. Beat butter, sugar, flour, cornstarch, and vanilla until smooth.
3. Pipe onto the sheet in swirls and bake for 12-15 min.
4. Once cool, sandwich with buttercream and jam.

Jaffa Cakes

Ingredients:

- 1/2 cup (100g) sugar
- 2 eggs
- 3/4 cup (100g) flour
- 1/2 cup (120g) orange jelly
- 1/2 cup (100g) dark chocolate

Instructions:

1. Preheat oven to 350°F (180°C). Grease a muffin tin.
2. Whisk eggs and sugar until pale. Fold in flour.
3. Spoon into tin and bake for 10 min.
4. Once cool, add a small disc of jelly on top.
5. Melt chocolate and coat each cake.

Bourbon Biscuits

Ingredients:

- 2 cups (250g) flour
- 1/2 cup (100g) sugar
- 1/4 cup (50g) cocoa powder
- 1/2 tsp baking soda
- 1/2 cup (115g) butter
- 2 tbsp golden syrup
- 2 tbsp milk

For filling:

- 1/4 cup (50g) butter
- 1/2 cup (100g) powdered sugar
- 1 tbsp cocoa powder

Instructions:

1. Preheat oven to 350°F (180°C). Line a baking sheet.
2. Mix flour, sugar, cocoa, and baking soda. Rub in butter, then add syrup and milk to form dough.
3. Roll out and cut into rectangles. Bake for 12-15 min.
4. Mix filling ingredients and sandwich between biscuits.

Custard Creams

Ingredients:

For the biscuits:

- 1 3/4 cups (220g) all-purpose flour
- 1/4 cup (30g) custard powder
- 1/2 cup (115g) butter, softened
- 1/2 cup (100g) sugar
- 1 egg
- 1 tsp vanilla extract

For the filling:

- 1/4 cup (50g) butter, softened
- 3/4 cup (100g) powdered sugar
- 1 tbsp custard powder
- 1 tbsp milk

Instructions:

1. Preheat oven to 350°F (180°C). Line a baking sheet.
2. Beat butter and sugar, then mix in egg and vanilla.
3. Stir in flour and custard powder to form a dough. Roll out and cut into small rectangles.
4. Bake for 10-12 minutes, then cool.
5. Mix filling ingredients, then sandwich between two biscuits.

Digestive Biscuits

Ingredients:

- 1 1/2 cups (180g) whole wheat flour
- 1/2 cup (60g) all-purpose flour
- 1/2 tsp baking soda
- 1/4 cup (50g) sugar
- 1/2 cup (115g) butter
- 2 tbsp milk

Instructions:

1. Preheat oven to 350°F (180°C). Line a baking sheet.
2. Mix flours, baking soda, and sugar. Rub in butter, then add milk to form a dough.
3. Roll out and cut into circles. Prick with a fork.
4. Bake for 12-15 minutes.

Rich Tea Biscuits

Ingredients:

- 2 cups (250g) all-purpose flour
- 1/2 tsp baking powder
- 1/4 cup (50g) butter
- 1/4 cup (50g) sugar
- 1/4 cup (60ml) milk

Instructions:

1. Preheat oven to 350°F (180°C). Line a baking sheet.
2. Mix flour and baking powder. Rub in butter, then add sugar and milk to form a dough.
3. Roll out and cut into circles. Prick with a fork.
4. Bake for 10-12 minutes.

Hobnobs

Ingredients:

- 1 cup (120g) rolled oats
- 1 cup (120g) whole wheat flour
- 1/2 tsp baking soda
- 1/2 cup (115g) butter
- 1/4 cup (50g) sugar
- 2 tbsp golden syrup

Instructions:

1. Preheat oven to 350°F (180°C). Line a baking sheet.
2. Mix oats, flour, and baking soda. Rub in butter, then add sugar and syrup to form a dough.
3. Roll into balls, flatten, and bake for 12-15 minutes.

Garibaldi Biscuits

Ingredients:

- 1 1/2 cups (180g) all-purpose flour
- 1/4 cup (50g) butter
- 1/4 cup (50g) sugar
- 1/4 cup (60ml) milk
- 3/4 cup (100g) currants

Instructions:

1. Preheat oven to 375°F (190°C). Line a baking sheet.
2. Rub butter into flour, then stir in sugar and milk to form a dough.
3. Roll out, scatter currants on half, fold over, and roll again.
4. Cut into strips and bake for 12-15 minutes.

Malt Loaf

Ingredients:

- 2 cups (250g) self-rising flour
- 1/2 cup (100g) brown sugar
- 1/2 cup (120g) malt extract
- 1/2 cup (120ml) tea
- 1 cup (150g) mixed dried fruit
- 1 egg

Instructions:

1. Preheat oven to 350°F (180°C). Grease a loaf tin.
2. Mix tea, malt extract, sugar, and dried fruit.
3. Stir in flour and beaten egg.
4. Pour into the tin and bake for 50-55 minutes.

Madeira Cake

Ingredients:

- 1 cup (225g) butter, softened
- 1 cup (200g) sugar
- 4 large eggs
- 2 cups (250g) self-rising flour
- Zest of 1 lemon
- 2 tbsp milk

Instructions:

1. Preheat oven to 350°F (180°C). Grease a loaf tin.
2. Beat butter and sugar, then mix in eggs.
3. Fold in flour, lemon zest, and milk.
4. Pour into the tin and bake for 45-50 minutes.

Lemon Drizzle Cake

Ingredients:

For the cake:

- 1 cup (225g) butter, softened
- 1 cup (200g) sugar
- 4 large eggs
- 2 cups (250g) self-rising flour
- Zest of 1 lemon

For the drizzle:

- Juice of 1 lemon
- 1/2 cup (100g) sugar

Instructions:

1. Preheat oven to 350°F (180°C). Grease a loaf tin.
2. Beat butter and sugar, then mix in eggs.
3. Fold in flour and lemon zest. Pour into tin and bake for 45 minutes.
4. Mix lemon juice and sugar, then pour over warm cake.

Carrot Cake

Ingredients:

- 1 cup (200g) brown sugar
- 3/4 cup (180ml) vegetable oil
- 3 eggs
- 2 cups (250g) all-purpose flour
- 1 tsp baking powder
- 1/2 tsp baking soda
- 1 tsp cinnamon
- 2 cups (200g) grated carrots
- 1/2 cup (75g) chopped walnuts

For the frosting:

- 1/2 cup (115g) butter, softened
- 1 cup (200g) cream cheese
- 2 cups (250g) powdered sugar

Instructions:

1. Preheat oven to 350°F (180°C). Grease a cake tin.
2. Mix sugar, oil, and eggs. Fold in flour, baking powder, soda, cinnamon, carrots, and walnuts.
3. Pour into tin and bake for 35-40 minutes.
4. Beat frosting ingredients and spread over the cooled cake.

Sticky Toffee Pudding

Ingredients:

For the cake:

- 1 cup (175g) dates, chopped
- 3/4 cup (180ml) boiling water
- 1 tsp baking soda
- 1/2 cup (115g) butter
- 3/4 cup (150g) brown sugar
- 2 eggs
- 1 1/4 cups (160g) self-rising flour

For the sauce:

- 1/2 cup (115g) butter
- 1 cup (200g) brown sugar
- 3/4 cup (180ml) heavy cream

Instructions:

1. Preheat oven to 350°F (180°C). Grease a baking dish.
2. Soak dates in boiling water with baking soda.
3. Cream butter and sugar, then beat in eggs. Fold in flour and soaked dates.
4. Pour into dish and bake for 35 minutes.
5. For the sauce, melt butter, sugar, and cream in a pan. Simmer for 5 minutes.
6. Pour warm sauce over pudding and serve.

Apple Crumble

Ingredients:

For the filling:

- 4 large apples, peeled, cored, and sliced
- 1/4 cup (50g) sugar
- 1 tsp cinnamon
- 1 tbsp lemon juice

For the crumble topping:

- 1 cup (125g) all-purpose flour
- 1/2 cup (100g) brown sugar
- 1/2 cup (115g) butter, cold and cubed
- 1/2 cup (50g) oats (optional)

Instructions:

1. Preheat oven to 375°F (190°C). Grease a baking dish.
2. Toss apples with sugar, cinnamon, and lemon juice, then spread in the dish.
3. Mix flour and sugar, then rub in butter until crumbly. Stir in oats if using.
4. Sprinkle over apples and bake for 30-35 minutes until golden.

Jam Roly-Poly

Ingredients:

- 2 cups (250g) self-rising flour
- 1/2 cup (115g) suet or butter
- 1/4 cup (50g) sugar
- 1/2 cup (120ml) milk
- 1/2 cup (150g) raspberry jam

Instructions:

1. Preheat oven to 375°F (190°C). Grease a baking dish.
2. Mix flour, suet (or butter), and sugar. Stir in milk to form a dough.
3. Roll out into a rectangle, spread with jam, then roll up.
4. Wrap loosely in parchment and foil, then bake for 40 minutes.

Spotted Dick

Ingredients:

- 2 cups (250g) self-rising flour
- 1/2 cup (115g) suet or butter
- 1/4 cup (50g) sugar
- 3/4 cup (100g) raisins or currants
- 3/4 cup (180ml) milk

Instructions:

1. Mix flour, suet (or butter), sugar, and raisins. Stir in milk to form a dough.
2. Shape into a log, wrap in parchment and foil, and steam for 1.5-2 hours.
3. Serve with custard.

Bread and Butter Pudding

Ingredients:

- 6 slices bread, buttered
- 1/2 cup (75g) raisins
- 2 cups (500ml) milk
- 1/2 cup (100g) sugar
- 2 eggs
- 1 tsp vanilla extract
- 1/2 tsp cinnamon

Instructions:

1. Preheat oven to 350°F (180°C). Grease a baking dish.
2. Layer buttered bread slices in the dish, sprinkling with raisins.
3. Heat milk and sugar until warm, then whisk in eggs, vanilla, and cinnamon.
4. Pour over the bread and let soak for 10 minutes.
5. Bake for 35-40 minutes until golden.

Queen of Puddings

Ingredients:

For the base:

- 2 cups (500ml) milk
- 1/2 cup (100g) sugar
- 1 cup (100g) breadcrumbs
- 1 tsp vanilla extract
- 2 egg yolks

For the topping:

- 1/2 cup (150g) raspberry jam
- 2 egg whites
- 1/4 cup (50g) sugar

Instructions:

1. Preheat oven to 350°F (180°C). Grease a baking dish.
2. Heat milk and sugar, then stir in breadcrumbs and vanilla. Let sit for 10 minutes.
3. Stir in egg yolks, then pour into the dish and bake for 20 minutes.
4. Spread jam over the baked base.
5. Whisk egg whites until stiff, then gradually add sugar.
6. Spoon meringue over the jam and bake for another 10 minutes until golden.

Tea Loaf

Ingredients:

- 2 cups (300g) mixed dried fruit
- 1 cup (240ml) strong tea
- 1/4 cup (50g) brown sugar
- 1 egg, beaten
- 2 cups (250g) self-rising flour
- 1 tsp cinnamon

Instructions:

1. Soak dried fruit in tea overnight.
2. Preheat oven to 350°F (180°C). Grease a loaf tin.
3. Stir in sugar, beaten egg, flour, and cinnamon to the soaked fruit.
4. Pour into the tin and bake for 45-50 minutes.

Fat Rascals

Ingredients:

- 2 cups (250g) self-rising flour
- 1/2 cup (100g) butter
- 1/4 cup (50g) sugar
- 1/4 cup (50g) candied peel, chopped
- 1/4 cup (50g) raisins
- 1 egg
- 1/4 cup (60ml) milk
- 1/4 tsp mixed spice (optional)

Instructions:

1. Preheat oven to 375°F (190°C). Line a baking sheet.
2. Rub butter into flour, then stir in sugar, candied peel, raisins, and spice.
3. Mix in egg and milk to form a dough.
4. Shape into round buns, place on the sheet, and bake for 15-20 minutes.

Banbury Cakes

Ingredients:

- 2 cups (250g) all-purpose flour
- 1/2 cup (115g) butter
- 1/4 cup (50g) sugar
- 1 tsp ground mixed spice
- 1/2 cup (75g) currants
- 1/2 cup (100g) glacé cherries, chopped
- 2 tbsp brandy or water

Instructions:

1. Preheat oven to 375°F (190°C). Grease a baking sheet.
2. Mix flour, butter, sugar, and mixed spice to form a dough.
3. Roll out and cut into circles, then fill with currants, cherries, and brandy.
4. Fold over, seal, and bake for 20-25 minutes.

Maids of Honour Tarts

Ingredients:

For the pastry:

- 1 1/2 cups (180g) all-purpose flour
- 1/2 cup (115g) butter
- 2 tbsp sugar
- 1 egg yolk
- 2 tbsp cold water

For the filling:

- 1/2 cup (100g) ricotta cheese
- 1/4 cup (50g) sugar
- 1 tbsp lemon juice
- 1 egg, beaten

Instructions:

1. Preheat oven to 375°F (190°C). Grease a muffin tin.
2. Mix flour, butter, and sugar. Stir in egg yolk and water to form a dough.
3. Roll out and line the muffin tin.
4. Mix ricotta, sugar, lemon juice, and egg, then spoon into pastry cases.
5. Bake for 15-18 minutes until golden.

Yorkshire Curd Tart

Ingredients:

For the pastry:

- 1 1/4 cups (160g) all-purpose flour
- 1/2 cup (115g) butter
- 2 tbsp sugar
- 1 egg yolk
- 1-2 tbsp cold water

For the filling:

- 1 1/2 cups (300g) curd cheese
- 1/4 cup (50g) sugar
- 2 tbsp lemon zest
- 1 egg, beaten
- 1 tbsp ground almonds
- 1 tbsp currants

Instructions:

1. Preheat oven to 350°F (180°C). Grease a tart tin.
2. Mix flour, butter, sugar, and egg yolk to form a dough. Roll out and line the tin.
3. Mix curd cheese, sugar, lemon zest, egg, ground almonds, and currants.
4. Pour into pastry shell and bake for 35-40 minutes until set.

Cornish Splits

Ingredients:

- 2 cups (250g) all-purpose flour
- 1/2 cup (115g) butter
- 1/4 cup (50g) sugar
- 1 tsp baking powder
- 1/2 cup (120ml) milk
- 1 egg
- 1/2 cup (75g) sultanas

Instructions:

1. Preheat oven to 375°F (190°C). Grease a baking sheet.
2. Rub butter into flour, then mix in sugar, baking powder, and sultanas.
3. Add milk and egg to form a dough.
4. Shape into buns and bake for 12-15 minutes until golden.

Ginger Snaps

Ingredients:

- 1 1/2 cups (190g) all-purpose flour
- 1/2 tsp baking soda
- 1 tsp ground ginger
- 1/2 tsp cinnamon
- 1/4 tsp ground cloves
- 1/2 cup (115g) butter
- 1/2 cup (100g) brown sugar
- 1/4 cup (60ml) molasses
- 1 egg

Instructions:

1. Preheat oven to 350°F (180°C). Line a baking sheet.
2. Mix flour, baking soda, and spices.
3. Beat butter, sugar, molasses, and egg, then stir in the dry ingredients.
4. Roll into balls, flatten, and bake for 8-10 minutes.

Brandy Snaps

Ingredients:

- 1/4 cup (50g) butter
- 1/2 cup (100g) brown sugar
- 1/4 cup (60ml) golden syrup
- 1 cup (120g) all-purpose flour
- 1 tsp ground ginger
- 1/4 tsp baking soda
- 1/4 cup (60ml) brandy (optional)

Instructions:

1. Preheat oven to 350°F (180°C). Line a baking sheet.
2. Melt butter, sugar, and golden syrup together.
3. Stir in flour, ginger, baking soda, and brandy.
4. Drop spoonfuls onto the sheet, bake for 5-7 minutes, and let cool.
5. Shape into curls or cones.

www.ingramcontent.com/pod-product-compliance
Lightning Source LLC
LaVergne TN
LVHW081332060526
838201LV00055B/2600